The
DISCIPLES'
COMPASS

A GUIDE TO
LIVING IN CHRIST

SCOTT WADE

PUBLISHED BY

MOMENTUM
—MINISTRIES—

Published by Momentum Ministries
The Disciples' Compass: A Guide to Living in Christ / Scott Wade

ISBN: 978-1-953285-79-9

Momentum Ministries
P.O. Box 206
Johns Island, SC 29457-0206

Cover and interior design by D.E. West—www.emoondesigns.com
with Dust Jacket Creative Services

Printed in the United States of America

MOMENTUM
—MINISTRIES—

www.momentumministries.org

DEDICATION

To Chad Johnson, my mentee and
friend who walked the trail of adversity
with me, imagining *The Essential Marks of a
Disciple*. Your loyalty and steadfast belief in
me came at just the right moment.
Thank you, Chad!

CONTENTS

"A word fitly spoken is like apples of gold in a setting of silver."
—Proverbs 25:11

PREFACE

For centuries explorers, sailors, and travelers have relied on the simple yet ingenious design of the compass to navigate the world. The earliest compasses, developed by the Chinese over a thousand years ago, were made using lodestone, a naturally magnetized mineral that mysteriously aligned itself with Earth's magnetic field. These early devices were suspended in water or set on a pivot, free to move in response to unseen forces that directed them toward true north.

As technology progressed, compasses became more refined. By the twelfth century, European navigators had adapted the floating lodestone into a needle-based design, where a thin strip of magnetized iron was mounted on a pivot. This allowed for greater precision and portability, making compasses essential tools for sailors venturing into the vast, uncharted seas.

A compass works because the earth itself is a giant magnet, with invisible lines of force stretching from pole to pole. The needle inside a compass aligns with these magnetic lines, always pointing toward magnetic north, helping travelers orient themselves and find their way.

Just as a compass aligns with Earth's magnetic field, our hearts must align with Christ if we are to walk in the right direction. When properly used, the Disciples' Compass keeps us from wandering aimlessly, pointing us to our True North—Jesus Christ.

ACKNOWLEDGMENTS

A dam Toler of Dust Jacket Press provided expert advice, publishing guidance, and design insight that helped shape this book. His expertise in the publishing process made this journey smoother, and I'm grateful for his support.

Jonathan Wright, my editor, once again worked his magic—cutting, pasting, rewording, and clarifying. His sharp eye for detail and clear grasp of my vision helped bring this book to life.

A special thanks to D. E. West, whose imagination and keen eye for what is appealing have provided clarity and impact.

The Board at Momentum Ministries—Aaron, Al, Irene, John, Joyce, Keith, and Tom—encouraged and guided me in all my ministry efforts while I was working on this book.

To those who pray, give, and volunteer with Momentum Ministries—you make this book and all our ministries possible. Your support fuels everything we do.

To my wife, Lana, whose steady presence, unwavering love, and encouragement have been a constant source of strength—not only in writing this book but in every step of life and ministry—her patience and faithfulness, even as I have quite honestly "failed" at retirement, have made all the difference.

To my children and grandchildren—your love, confidence, and joy continue to inspire me and bring meaning to the work God has called me to do. Thank you for being part of this journey too!

INTRODUCTION

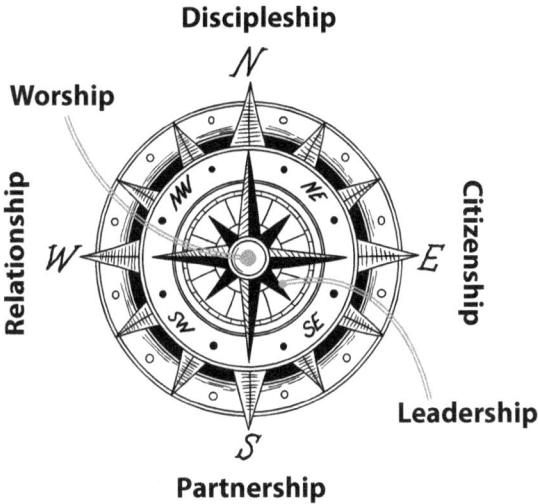

Discipleship

Worship

Relationship

Citizenship

Leadership

Partnership

There's an old saying that goes, "If you don't know where you're going, any road will take you there." But for the disciple of Jesus Christ the destination is clear—Christlikeness. The challenge, however, is navigating the journey. Life presents countless distractions, detours, and dangers that can lead us off course. What landmarks are available to us? How do we stay oriented? How do we ensure that we are following Jesus faithfully and growing into His likeness?

The answer lies in the Disciples' Compass.

The Call to Discipleship

In Matthew 28:18–20 Jesus gives His followers a clear mission:

> "All authority in heaven and on earth has been given to me. Go therefore and make disciples of all nations, baptizing them in the name of the Father and of the Son and of the Holy Spirit, teaching them to observe all that I have commanded you. And behold, I am with you always, to the end of the age."

Jesus did not call us to make Christians—He alone makes Christians when people choose to follow Him. Nor did He command us to make saints—God alone sanctifies His people. He did not say to make brothers or sisters—we become part of the family of God through spiritual birth, not human effort. He did not say to make believers—faith is a personal response to God's grace, a gift indeed, but from God and not us.

What Jesus did call us to make is *disciples*!

The Greek verb form of *disciple* means—

1. To be a disciple of someone and to follow his or her teachings and precepts.

2. To make a disciple by teaching and instruction.

The noun form simply means "learner," "pupil," or "follower." It refers to those who have chosen to follow Jesus, embracing His teachings and living according to His example. A disciple is one who follows Jesus in a disciplined way, undergoing a process of transformation.

Why the Compass?

A compass is an essential tool for travelers, ensuring that they stay on course. The Disciples' Compass serves the same purpose in our spiritual journey, marking six key points that define and direct a Disciples' life:

1. Know God in Worship (Pivot Point)
2. Show Love in Relationship (West Point)
3. Grow Up in Discipleship (North Point)
4. Go Out in Citizenship (East Point)
5. Sow Seeds of Partnership (South Point)
6. Flow On to Leadership (Point of Impact)

Each of these compass points—or marks of a disciple of Jesus Christ—is crucial. Without worship our lives lack a true center. Without relationship we lose accountability and encouragement. Without discipleship we remain spiritually stagnant. Without citizenship we fail to live out Christ in the world. Without partnership we neglect our role in supporting the church. And without leadership we miss the opportunity to fulfill the Great Commission

Each chapter in this book will explore one of the compass points, offering biblical insights, real-life applications, and reflection questions to help you integrate these principles into your daily life.

Are you ready to embark on this journey of following Jesus? Let's take the first step—by centering our lives through worship.

ONE

KNOW GOD IN WORSHIP

A Story of Worship: Handel's *Messiah*

In the year 1741 composer George Frideric Handel was struggling. He was deeply in debt, facing poor health, and on the verge of losing everything. Then something remarkable happened. A friend gave him a collection of scriptures compiled into a libretto, focusing on the life and mission of Jesus Christ. Inspired by these words, Handel locked himself in his study and composed one of the greatest musical masterpieces of all time—*Messiah*—in just twenty-four days. When he completed the famous "Hallelujah Chorus," he is said to have exclaimed, "I did think I did see all heaven before me, and the great God Himself!"

The first performance of *Messiah* was met with overwhelming praise, and when it was later performed before King George II, it is said that the king himself stood in worship during the "Hallelujah" chorus—a tradition that continues to this day.

Handel's story is a testimony to the centrality and power of worship—how surrendering to God's presence will transform despair into joy and struggle into praise.

Knowing God in Worship

Worship is the pivot point of the Disciples' Compass because everything in our relationship with God through Jesus Christ revolves around it. It is at the beginning of our journey and informs our identity. Jesus declares—

> "The hour is coming, and is now here, when the true worshipers will worship the Father in spirit and truth, for the Father is seeking such people to worship him." (John 4:23)

Notice those words: "The Father is *seeking* such people." He is actively seeking you! God is not indifferent about your worship because it is to be the center of your life. He desires worshipers who truly know Him and reverence Him, who worship in spirit and in truth. Worship is not a ritual or routine; it is an encounter with the living God, who has come to you.

Imagine the creator of the universe seeking you, drawing you into His presence to worship Him. Right now, pause—lift your heart in gratitude, adore His majesty, and let worship rise from the depths of your soul.

True worship is not just a human action but is also a response to a divine impulse, to the love and grace of Jesus Christ. It is through Christ that we come to know God and enter into worship that is both Spirit-filled and truth-driven. Nor is worship just an event—it is the continual outflow of a life captured by Jesus.

Call to Worship

Christian worship services often begin with a "call to worship," the implication being that in order to experience worship we must first answer the call to worship. So too, if we are to live lives of worship, we must answer that first call to worship—the call to begin following Jesus.

We answer that call when we . . . *admit, believe,* and *confess.* When we do that, our sins are forgiven, we are given new life in Christ, we become true (genuine, sincere) worshipers of God, with Christ taking His place in the center of our lives!

The ABCs of a Personal Relationship With Jesus Christ

A—Admit that you have sinned.
  All have sinned and fall short of the glory of God (Romans 3:23 NIV).

B—Believe that Jesus Christ died for you.
  To all who did receive him, to those who believed in his name, he gave the right to become children of God (John 1:12 NIV).

C—Confess Jesus Christ as Lord of *your* life.
  If you confess with your mouth that Jesus is Lord and believe in your heart that

*God raised him from the dead, you
will be saved. For with the heart one be-
lieves and is justified, and with the mouth
one confesses and is saved.*
(Romans 1:9–10).

Pray "the sinner's prayer"—

"Dear Lord Jesus, I know that I am a sinner. I
believe that you died for my sins and arose
from the grave. I now turn from my sins and
invite you to come into my heart and life. I
receive you as my personal Savior and follow
you as my Lord. Amen."

Be assured of your salvation:

*"Here I am! I stand at the door and knock.
If anyone hears my voice and opens the
door, I will come in and eat with him, and
he with me"* (Revelation 3:20 NIV).

*And this is the testimony: God has given
us eternal life, and this life is in his Son. He
who has the Son has life; he who does not
have the Son of God does not have life*
(1 John 5:11–12 NIV).

Adapted from Stan Toler, *ABCs of Evangelism*
Used by permission

Call to Surrender:
A Life Fully Devoted to God

A life of worship—a life centered on God—starts in earnest when we are saved. But there is more. Jesus said that the greatest commandment is to love God completely—with all our hearts and souls and minds and strength. A life of worship, therefore, continues as we **fully surrender our lives** to God. Just as **justification** is the moment we place our faith in Christ for salvation, **sanctification** is the ongoing transformation of our hearts and lives into the likeness of Jesus. Entire sanctification is the **deepest act of worship**—fully yielding ourselves to God's will, being set apart for His purposes, the Holy Spirit "purifying [our] hearts by faith" (Acts 15:9 KJV).

Paul urges believers toward this kind of complete surrender:

> I appeal to you therefore, brothers, by the mercies of God, to present your bodies as a living sacrifice, holy and acceptable to God, which is your spiritual worship. (Romans 12:1)

To worship God fully is to **offer every part of ourselves**—our desires, our plans, our very lives—into His hands. It is not merely a moment; it is a lifestyle of worship, walking in the power of the Holy Spirit, free from the grip of sin and fully alive to God. This is what John Wesley described as being **"perfected in love"**—in which our hearts, minds, and actions are fully yielded to God, and we live in obedience, not out of duty but out of love.

What does it mean to be entirely sanctified?

- *A complete surrender*—not just turning from sin but giving every part of our lives to Christ.

- *The Holy Spirit's work*—Entire sanctification is not self-improvement; it is the Spirit filling us and refining us.

- *A life set apart*—It means living holy, not by our strength but through God's grace.

- *Freedom in Christ*—The chains of self-centeredness are broken, and love becomes our motive.

- *A heart of worship*—Our daily lives become testimonies of God's transforming power.

Are you ready to surrender and be filled with the Spirit?

How to Be Filled with the Holy Spirit

O—Offer yourself completely to God.
Offer your bodies as a living sacrifice, holy and pleasing to God—this is your true and proper worship (Romans 12:1 NIV).

A—Ask for the gift of the Holy Spirit.
"How much more will the heavenly Father give the Holy Spirit to those who ask him!" (Luke 11:13).

6

O—Obey God. Are you saying yes to all of what God says yes to and no to all He says no to?
We are witnesses to these things, and so is the Holy Spirit, whom God has given to those who obey him (Acts 5:32).

B—Believe that God sanctifies you and fills you with His Holy Spirit.
"God, who knows the heart, bore witness to them, by giving them the Holy Spirit just as he did to us, and he made no distinction between us and them, having cleansed their hearts by faith" (Acts 15:8–9).

Lord, I offer my whole life to you. Sanctify me completely. Fill me with your Spirit. May I live fully surrendered, walking in holiness and love. Amen.

Adapted from Lenny Wisehart,
You've Got His Word on It
Used by permission

May the God of peace himself sanctify you completely, and may your whole spirit and soul and body be kept blameless at the coming of our Lord Jesus Christ (1 Thessalonians 5:23).

An Elevated View of Worship

With our lives centered on Jesus, completely surrendered to Him, we discover that our worship cannot be confined to church services or songs or even personal devotions but is reflected in how we live each day. Worship is an ongoing act of devotion to God, both privately and publicly.

Here are just a few of the things that constitute being a worshiper of God:

- Continual awareness of God's presence and activity in our lives: "Whoever would draw near to God must believe that he exists and that he rewards those who seek him" (Hebrews 11:6).

- Reverence and awe—Worship begins when we have a profound sense of God's holiness and our dependence on Jesus Christ.

- Joy and celebration—Worship is an expression of our delight in the Lord through Jesus Christ.

- Obedience—Worship is not just exuberant singing and joyous expressions of praise; it is a state of complete surrender to the teachings of the Bible and the will of Jesus.

- Sacrifice—True worship requires laying something down before God, following Christ's example of self-giving love. Remember these words of Israel's King David: "I will not offer burnt offerings to the Lord my God that cost me nothing" (2 Samuel 24:24).

- Walking with the Spirit—Worship includes daily communion with the Holy Spirit, walking in step with Him, and allowing Him to lead and transform us.

Practical Expressions of Worship

- Daily prayer and Scripture reading—setting aside time to commune with God.
- Singing or listening to worship music—filling our hearts with songs of praise.
- Serving others as an act of worship—seeing our actions as a way to glorify God.
- Expressing gratitude—developing a heart of thanksgiving in all circumstances.
- Living in obedience—making decisions that align with God's will and character.
- Testifying—telling others what God has done for you.

Reflection and Application

1. Reflect: How does my daily life reflect worship beyond Sunday services?
2. Ask: Can I think of other expressions of worship?
3. Act: Identify one act of worship you can offer God this week—whether through prayer, service, or surrender.
4. Pray: Ask God to cultivate in you a heart of worship that remains steadfast in both peace and trial, always anchored in Jesus Christ.

TWO

SHOW LOVE IN RELATIONSHIP

A Story of Relationship: The Power of Friendship

In 1914 during World War I, two soldiers, best friends since childhood, fought side by side in the trenches of France. During a fierce battle one of them was wounded and left stranded in no-man's-land. The other, safely behind the lines, asked permission to go and rescue his friend. His officer refused, warning him that it was too dangerous. But against orders the soldier went anyway. When he returned, carrying his dying friend, the officer was furious. "I told you it wasn't worth it!" he scolded. The soldier replied, "It *was* worth it, sir. When I got there he was still alive, and he said, 'I knew you'd come.'"

True relationship means standing by each other even in the hardest of times. Jesus said,

> "Greater love has no one than this, that someone lay down his life for his friends." (John 15:13)

Showing Love in Relationship

As the needle of the disciples' compass revolves around its pivot point, it aligns us with four other points—west, north, east, and south. Worship is depicted as the pivot point, but what is indicated by the other points of our disciples' compass?

Let's start with the west point: Christian relationship. West is symbolically seen as a horizontal direction on a compass, indicating how we live God's love outward in community. This horizontal focus prepares us for the other horizontal dimension: east, which depicts citizenship. Before we turn our love "outside" the church, we must learn to walk in Christlike relationship with fellow believers. And we discover that these relationships are essential for spiritual growth.

Jesus Himself modeled the importance of relationship, investing deeply in His disciples and teaching them to love one another as He loved them. In the days following Pentecost, the early believers in Jerusalem experienced an unprecedented sense of that unity:

> So those who received his word were baptized, and there were added that day about three thousand souls. And they devoted themselves to the apostles' teaching and the fellowship, to the breaking of bread and the prayers. And awe came upon every soul, and many wonders and signs were being done through the apostles. And all who believed were together and had all things in common. And they were selling their

possessions and belongings and distributing the proceeds to all, as any had need. And day by day, attending the temple together and breaking bread in their homes, they received their food with glad and generous hearts, praising God and having favor with all the people. And the Lord added to their number day by day those who were being saved. (Acts 2:41–47)

This early church community exemplified what it means to walk in relationship—not just with God but also with one another. They did not live isolated spiritual lives; instead, their faith was deeply communal, marked by love, generosity, and mutual encouragement.

The Command to Love

> "A new commandment I give to you,
> that you love one another."
> (John 13:34)

Love is not simply an idea—it is action. It is laying down our lives for one another, just as Jesus laid down His life for us:

By this we know love, that he laid down his life for us, and we ought to lay down our lives for the brothers. But if anyone has the world's goods and sees his

brother in need, yet closes his heart
against him, how does God's love abide
in him? Little children, let us not love in
word or talk but in deed and in truth. (1
John 3:16–18)

Further, for love to be real, there must be an object to
that love—even when the very ones we are called to love
make loving difficult, seemingly impossible. Jesus never
gives an impossible command. His grace enables us to love
as He has loved us:

God's love has been poured out into
our hearts through the Holy Spirit, who
has been given to us. (Romans 5:5 NIV)

The Community of Love

**"As I have loved you,
so you must love one another."
(John 13:34 NIV)**

Christian community is built on the love we show one
another. Our relationships serve as a testimony to the
watching world. How we love our families, fellow believers,
and even those who challenge us reflects the love of Christ.
Our love within the church must be like Jesus's love:

- Unusual—It stands out from the way the world
  loves.

- Unnatural—It is not based on feelings but on commitment.

- Unrelenting—It does not give up when relationships are hard.

- Unconditional—It is not based on what others do for us.

- Unlimited—It does not run out, for it is sourced in Christ Himself.

The Communication of Love

> "By this all people will know that you are my disciples, if you have love for one another."
> (John 13:35)

We often seek to impress the world through sound doctrine, morality, and good works. While these are important, Jesus says the defining mark of His disciples is love within the church. When we love one another in a way that reflects Christ, we communicate something that is often missing in the world. This love draws others toward us and ultimately toward Him. Conversely, when we fail to love in this way, we communicate another message to outsiders, that here's a group no one wants to be a part of. This is why our love for one another is tied directly to our mission.

> Loving relationships are the bridge over which the gospel travels.

If we want to make disciples, we must first live as disciples—marked by radical, Christ-centered love. Our relationships are a direct reflection of our discipleship. If we claim to follow Jesus, we must also commit to loving others as He does.

What Relationship in Christ Looks Like

> Bear one another's burdens, and so fulfill the law of Christ (Galatians 6:2).

> Let us consider how to stir up one another to love and good works, not neglecting to meet together, as is the habit of some, but encouraging one another, and all the more as you see the Day drawing near (Hebrews 10:24–25).

> Two are better than one, because they have a good reward for their toil. For if they fall, one will lift up his fellow. But woe to him who is alone when he falls and has not another to lift him up! (Ecclesiastes 4:9–10).

The Elements of Christian Relationship

1. Love and sacrifice—Jesus demonstrated the highest form of love through His sacrifice. We are called to lay down our own desires to love others selflessly.

2. Encouragement and strengthening—The Christian life is not meant to be lived alone. We need one an-

other for encouragement, prayer, and mutual edification.

3. Forgiveness and reconciliation—Just as Christ has forgiven us, we are to extend grace and forgiveness to others.

4. Shared mission—Relationships in Christ are not just about friendship but also about walking together in God's mission, making disciples and spreading His love.

5. Bearing one another's burdens—As Paul wrote in Galatians 6:2, we fulfill the law of Christ when we help carry each other's struggles and burdens.

Practical Expressions of Relationship

True relationships are not about breadth but about depth. Social media and casual acquaintances make for a wide network, but Christian relationships go deep—marked by shared lives, sacrificial love, and intentional kindness.

With that in mind, here are some ways to live out biblical relationships:

-   Join or form a small group or Bible study together. Fellowship and shared learning strengthen your faith.

-   Pray for one another. Interceding for a brother or sister deepens spiritual bonds.

-   Call on your brother or sister. A simple call or message can encourage someone in need. Follow the prompts that you feel from the Holy Spirit as you are praying for your friends.

- When possible, pay a personal visit to those in need. Your personal presence brings the actual presence of Christ into the setting.

- Share your means. Meeting physical needs is a tangible expression of Christ's love.

Reflection and Application

1. Reflect: Who in your life has encouraged you in your faith journey? How can you strengthen those relationships?

2. Ask: Am I missing out on relationships within the church that would benefit both me and others?

3. Act: Reach out to someone this week—whether through a call, a meal, or an encouraging message—and build deeper Christian fellowship.

4. Pray: Ask God to help you grow in love, patience, and forgiveness as you cultivate godly relationships.

Are you ready to grow in love? Relationship is not just an aspect of the Christian life; it is at the very heart of how we reflect Christ to the world.

THREE

GROW UP IN DISCIPLESHIP

A Story of Discipleship: The Training of Apprentices

In the Renaissance era Leonardo da Vinci was not only one of the greatest artists and inventors in history but also a mentor to young apprentices. One of his most famous students, Francesco Melzi, initially had no artistic training, but under da Vinci's guidance, he became an accomplished painter and actually helped preserve much of da Vinci's work for future generations. Da Vinci didn't just teach technique—he taught discipline, curiosity, and a way of thinking that shaped Melzi's entire life.

Discipleship is not just about knowledge but is also about transformation through common experiences and shared wisdom. Like da Vinci with his apprentices, Jesus calls us to be His disciples, shaping us into His likeness through teaching, relationship, and application.

Growing Up in Discipleship

Worship is our pivot point and relationship is the west point, horizontal as viewed on a compass. Discipleship can be seen as a vertical point—and on a compass it is upward, indicating that we grow *up* in the pursuit of Christlikeness.

We are called to mature in our faith, not staying stagnant but deepening our knowledge, obedience, and love for God. In Luke 2:52 we see that even Jesus experienced growth:

> **Jesus grew in wisdom and stature,**
> **and in favor with God and man.**
> **(Luke 2:52 NIV)**

The Greek word for *grow* used here is *prokopto,* which means "to beat forward" or "to lengthen out by hammering," as a blacksmith forges metal. This suggests that growth is not effortless but requires discipline, intentionality, and endurance.

Interestingly, Luke could have used other Greek words for growth:

- *Mekyno*: natural, organic growth like that of plants

- *Auxano:* spontaneous, self-sustained growth

- *Ginomai*: arising, evolving, or coming into existence

These three words indicate a passive growth, something that happens without effort. *Prokopto,* however, emphasizes strenuous effort and perseverance.

If Jesus Himself grew through intentional, disciplined effort, how much more should we? Our growth as disciples is not automatic but rather intentional.

Growing in Wisdom, Stature, and Favor

Jesus's growth as described in Luke 2:52 provides a model for our own discipleship journey. Let's consider them in turn.

Growing in Wisdom

> The fear of the Lord is the beginning of wisdom,
> and the knowledge of the Holy One is insight.
> (Proverbs 9:10)

Growing in wisdom is what I would call classical Christian growth. It's what we tend to think of when we think of discipleship.

Wisdom—*sophia*. This kind of wisdom is obtained through—

- Study
- Open-mindedness
- Attention
- Observation
- Training
- "Trellising" (Think of shaping a plant by encouraging it to grow in a particular direction or shape.)

Those things aren't easy!

Growing in Stature

> **Like newborn infants, long for the pure spiritual milk, that by it you may grow up into salvation.**
> **(1 Peter 2:2)**

The word *stature* is *helikia*—and can mean "increasing"—

- In *age*

- In *size*

- Then by metaphor—in *maturity*

Luke's emphasis is not on Jesus's age—not based on the word He chose to depict growth. It also is not on physical size because we cannot determine how tall we will end up just by willing ourselves to be taller. What Luke was concerned about—and what we need to understand—is the metaphorical use of *helikia*. As Jesus aged, He matured. Some people grow bigger and older but do not mature in character!

Growing in Favor with God

> **Draw near to God, and he will draw near to you.**
> **(James 4:8)**

Growth—even Christian growth—is not for growth's sake alone. You don't get bigger just to be bigger. God has a plan and purpose for you.

The word for *favor* is *charis*, and it means grace, good will, favor. It comes from the verb that means "to rejoice." Jesus grew in favor with God. He made God rejoice. Do you remember what God said of Jesus when He was baptized? "This is my Son, whom I love. With Him I am well pleased." Isn't it exciting to think that we can make the heart of God rejoice as we grow in worship, in Christlikeness, in service, and in leadership?

Growing in Favor with Man

> "Let your light shine before others,
> so that they may see your good works and give
> glory to your Father who is in heaven."
> (Matthew 5:16)

Jesus's growth in favor was not just with God. It was also with man. While Jesus said that we would sometimes be hated because of Him, while we may be rejected and persecuted, we know that a follower of Christ is ultimately a better person to be around. We see this favor particularly in the arenas of

- Citizenship
- Christian relationship
- Partnership
- Leadership

Practical Expressions of Discipleship

Since growing in discipleship is not passive but active, it is appropriate to ask, "What can I *do* to grow?"

- Daily Bible study and prayer—rooting yourself in God's Word and presence in your life

- Memorizing scripture—hiding God's Word in your heart

- Applying biblical truth—living out what you learn

- Connecting to a group—learning and growing from the strengths and struggles of others

- Following a mentor—partnering with a mature believer

- Teaching others—passing on the faith

Reflection and Application

1. Reflect: Look at the list above. How are you experiencing growth through those areas? Is your life changing or just your knowledge?

2. Ask: Am I growing in wisdom? In maturity? In nearness to God? In value for my community?

3. Act: Identify one area in which you need to mature spiritually and take steps to grow.

4. Pray: Ask God to reveal relationships and practices that will cultivate spiritual growth and follow up on what you hear.

Are you ready to grow? Discipleship is the call to become more like Christ—learning, obeying, and teaching others to do the same.

FOUR

GO OUT IN CITIZENSHIP

A Story of Citizenship: William Wilberforce and the Fight for Justice

In 18th-century England William Wilberforce was a rising politician with a promising career ahead. But after a profound spiritual conversion, he wrestled with whether he should leave politics to pursue full-time ministry. Seeking counsel, he was encouraged by John Newton, the former slave trader turned preacher, to remain where God had placed him—in Parliament—so that he could bring Christian influence into national affairs. Wilberforce committed his life to living out his faith as a citizen of both heaven and earth. He spent decades leading the fight against the British slave trade, facing fierce opposition and personal struggles. In 1807, after years of perseverance, the Abolition of the Slave Trade Act was passed, ending the legal slave trade in Britain.

Wilberforce's story exemplifies what it means to be a citizen of both the kingdom of God and the world, using one's influence, career, and daily life to live out God's purposes.

Going Out in Citizenship

With the mark of citizenship, we are once again on a horizontal aspect. This movement is depicted in the east point of the compass.

Jesus—the Son of God—denied Himself to go where His Father wanted Him to go. The Bible says that Jesus left behind all the glories of heaven and became a citizen of this world!

> Your attitude should be the same as that of Christ Jesus: Who, being in very nature God, did not consider equality with God something to be grasped, but made himself nothing, taking the very nature of a servant, being made in human likeness. And being found in appearance as a man, he humbled himself and became obedient to death—even death on a cross. (Philippians 2:5–8 NIV)

Think about it—Jesus, the eternal Son of God, became a citizen of planet Earth in order to follow where God was leading Him. How can we expect to do anything less? If I choose to follow Jesus, I will need to deny myself to go where God wants me to go too.

The Call to "Go"—Biblical Examples

God has always been in the business of sending His people into the world as citizens with a mission:

- To Abraham—"Go . . . to the land I will show you" (Genesis 12:1 NIV).

- To Moses—"So now, go" (Exodus 3:10 NIV).

- To Isaiah—"Whom shall I send? And who will go for us?" (Isaiah 6:8).

- To the disciples—"Go. . . . I am sending you out" (Luke 10:3).

- To Paul—"Go. . . . I will send you far away" (Acts 22:21).

- To the disciples—"All authority in heaven and on earth has been given to me. Therefore go and make disciples of all nations, baptizing them in the name of the Father and of the Son and of the Holy Spirit, and teaching them to obey everything I have commanded you. And surely I am with you always, to the very end of the age" (Matthew 28:18-20 NIV).

Where Are We to Go?
Living as Citizens in Every Sphere

Where do we live out our Christian citizenship? Luke, the physician and gospel writer, gives us a broad picture:

- Home and family—If following Jesus doesn't make me a better husband, wife, parent, or child, then how closely am I really following Him?

- Community—Involvement in community service, compassionate ministries, and outreach should be part of our DNA as Spirit-filled followers of Jesus.

- Workplace—A follower of Christ should be the most diligent, ethical, and honorable worker in any organization.

- Among those different from us—We reach across racial, religious, economic, ideological, and political lines to reflect Christ's love.

- The ends of the earth—Jesus calls us to all nations, meaning that our faith affects our response to global issues like immigration, the environment, and world missions.

> **"Let your light shine before others,
> so that they may see your good works and give
> glory to your Father who is in heaven."
> (Matthew 5:16)**

Practical Expressions of Citizenship

How do you live as a citizen of God's kingdom while engaging in the world?

- Live out your faith at home and around friends.
- Be involved in your community.
- Live with integrity in your workplace.
- Support missions and evangelism.
- Vote and participate in society responsibly. Use your influence to reflect God's values.

- Engage in acts of justice and mercy. Care for the vul nerable, advocate for righteousness.

Reflection and Application

1. Reflect: How do you see your role as a citizen of both God's kingdom and the world?

2. Ask: Can I say with sincerity that I am the best spouse, worker, neighbor, friend I can be with the help of God? If not, what can I do to become such?

3. Act: Identify one way you can live out your faith more sincerely in your home, work, or community.

4. Pray: Ask God to open doors for you to be salt and light where He has placed you.

Are you ready to go? Citizenship is not just a privilege— it's a responsibility to bring Christ's love and truth wherever He sends us!

FIVE

SOW SEEDS OF PARTNERSHIP

A Story of Partnership: Paul and the Philippians

Unlike some of the other churches Paul planted, the Philippian church consistently stood by him in partnership, supporting him spiritually and materially—even when he was imprisoned. So great was the experience of *koinonia* (Greek for "partnership" or "fellowship") that Paul wrote—

> I thank my God in all my remembrance of you, always in every prayer of mine for you all making my prayer with joy, because of your partnership in the gospel from the first day until now. (Philippians 1:3–5)

The Philippian church was formed when a businesswoman in the community accepted Christ and immediately partnered with Paul in the work of the gospel, opening her home to host the fledgling congregation. That partnership would soon be tested, however. Paul and his missionary companion, Silas, were beaten and imprisoned after casting out a demon from a slave girl (Acts 16:16–24). Instead of despairing, they prayed and sang hymns, and God miraculously opened the prison doors. This event led to the conversion of the Philippian jailer and his household, strengthening the influence of the church in that city. Years later when Paul was in another imprisonment, the Philippians did not abandon him. Instead, they sent Epaphroditus to bring financial aid and encouragement. Paul wrote to them—

> It was kind of you to share my trouble. And you Philippians yourselves know that in the beginning of the gospel, when I left Macedonia, no church entered into partnership with me in giving and receiving, except you only. (Philippians 4:14–15)

The Philippians lived out true partnership—not just in giving but also in praying, serving, and standing with Paul in both joy and suffering. Their story challenges us to become partners in God's work, just as they were.

Sowing Seeds of Partnership

When we sow seeds we generally think of planting them *down* in the ground. On the compass the south point is perceived as downward.

Partnership in the church is about more than attending services—it's about active engagement in God's mission. We partner with God and one another in four essential ways: praying, serving, inviting, and giving.

Partnering through Prayer

> **The prayer of a righteous person has
> great power as it is working.
> (James 5:16)**

As a believer, you should cultivate these prayer partnerships:

- Your partnership with God—a daily, personal relationship with Him

- Your partnerships at home—praying for and with family members

- Your partnerships in church—interceding for fellow believers and church leadership

- God's partnership with you—trusting that God is at work in and through your prayers

Partnering through Service

One of the most powerful ways to partner in the church is by serving. We see a compelling example in Luke 5 when Jesus calls Peter to a new kind of service:

- **My "Stuff" Really Belongs to God**
  He got into one of the boats, the one belonging

to Simon, and asked him to put out a little from shore. Then he sat down and taught the people from the boat. (Luke 5:3–4 NIV)

Who owns your resources, time, and talents—you or God?

- **Working on My Own Is Fruitless and Exhausting**

  "Master, we've worked hard all night and haven't caught anything. But because you say so, I will let down the nets." (Luke 5:5 NIV)

  Service apart from God's leading often results in frustration.

- **God-Given Strengths Yield Abundant Results**

  When they had done so, they caught such a large number of fish that their nets began to break. (Luke 5:6 NIV)

  Serving in God's strength brings supernatural results.

- **Letting God Set the Agenda Is Always Best**

  Then Jesus said to Simon, "Don't be afraid; from now on you will fish for people." So they pulled their boats up on shore, left everything and followed him. (Luke 5:10–11 NIV)

  True service means trusting God's plan over our own.

Partnering through Invitation

> Go out to the highways and hedges and compel
> people to come in, that my house may be filled.
> (Luke 14:23)

Have you considered that when you do not invite people to Christ and His church, you are failing to invite *Him*? Inviting others to faith is not optional—it is a core part of our partnership with God.

Partnering through Giving

> Each one must give as he has decided in
> his heart, not reluctantly or under compulsion,
> for God loves a cheerful giver.
> (2 Corinthians 9:7)

Generosity is another key expression of partnership. Consider these opportunities for Christian stewardship:

- Tithing—giving 10 percent of your income through the local church

- Church offerings—special giving for God's glory and others' good

- Supporting ministries—partnering financially with missions and evangelism efforts

- Compassionate giving—helping those in crisis or need

- Anonymous gifts of blessing—giving without recognition, simply to bless others

Practical Expressions of Partnership

How can we actively sow seeds of partnership?

- Commit to a prayer group—Join a group that prays for your church and community.

- Find a place to serve—Use your talents and time in ministry. Don't wait to be asked, but present yourself first to God, then the church as a laborer in His work.

- Invite someone to church—Reach out to a friend, neighbor, or coworker.

- Give generously—Support missions, ministries, and those in need.

Reflection and Application

Reflect: How am I currently partnering with God and others in His mission?

1. Ask: Do I see myself as a partner in the work of God? Do I see the value of partnerships in the gospel? What can I do to change my perspective?

2. Act: Identify one area—prayer, service, invitation, or giving—where you can take a new step of faith. Then do it!

3. Pray: Ask God to show you how to become a stronger partner in His kingdom work.

Are you ready to partner with God and His church? Just as with the Philippians with Paul, we are called to actively participate in God's mission, standing together in prayer, service, invitation, and generosity!

SIX

FLOW ON TO LEADERHSIP

A Story of Leadership:
John Wesley and the Methodists

In the 1700s John Wesley had no intention of starting a movement. He simply wanted to disciple people and deepen their walk with Christ. However, his methodical approach to spiritual growth led to the formation of Methodist societies, small groups of believers who met regularly to encourage one another in faith.

Wesley didn't just preach sermons—he trained leaders. He created a system in which new believers were discipled and in time became disciple-makers themselves. This multiplication of leaders eventually fueled a revival that swept across England and America, shaping Christian history.

Regarding Wesley's ability to disciple and retain converts, his contemporary George Whitefield wrote this: "My brother Wesley acted wisely—the souls that were awakened under his ministry he joined in class, and thus preserved the fruits of his labor. This I neglected, and my people are a rope of sand."

Wesley's model shows us that Christian leadership isn't about titles—it's about influence and preservation. Every believer is called to lead others to Christ.

Flowing on to Leadership

At this point you may be wondering, "Okay, I understand the four directional points of a compass and even the pivot point, but what in the world is the sixth point?" It is the "point" of the compass itself—leading us on a journey. In our model it is depicted by the arrow, which indicates movement away from the compass. As we move along the path of Christlikeness, we quickly notice that there are those before us, those beside us, and those behind us.

Knowing our bearings is not the end point of the disciples' compass. Every child of God is called to keep moving—upward, onward, and outward. We shouldn't just point ourselves in a direction; we need to move in that direction. As we do, we discover that God transforms us from followers into leaders. All of us are leaders because all of us have people behind us on the discipleship path. As we follow Christ, we are leading them closer to Jesus.

> **"Follow me, and I will make you fishers of men."**
> **(Matthew 4:19)**

I used to divide people into leaders and followers, reserving the term *leaders* for those in specific positions of authority in the church. But I don't do that anymore. For no matter where we are in the organizational structure of the church, we are all leaders—pointing others to Jesus, influencing their faith. Two key questions help us evaluate our leadership journey:

Who is discipling me?
Who am I discipling?

All followers of Jesus Christ are leaders. No matter where we are in our journey with Christ, someone is "behind" us. So we are called to make disciples—helping others come closer to Jesus.

The Making of Christ-Followers

Disciples are . . .
- **Spirit-made**
- **Self-made**
- **Sacramentally made**
- **Socially made**

As you fulfill Jesus's commission to make disciples, you may want to keep in mind these four ways that disciples are made:

1. **Christ-followers are Spirit-made**

Salvation is the work of the Holy Spirit. We do not make ourselves followers of Christ—He calls us, convicts us, and transforms us.

"No one can come to me unless the Father who sent me draws him." (John 6:44)

2. **Christ-followers are self-made**

While God initiates salvation, spiritual growth requires personal effort. Discipleship takes intentionality. In addition to this, we must remember that we cannot make disciples without the effort of the one being discipled.

Train yourself for godliness. (1 Timothy 4:7)

3. **Christ-followers are sacramentally made**

The sacraments remind us that discipleship is not just personal but also communal.

- Baptism—a public declaration of faith, a rite of initiation

- The Lord's Supper—regular participation in Christ's body, a rite of sanctification

4. **Christ-followers are socially made**

Discipleship thrives in community. Some examples of social groups that enhance spiritual growth include the following:

- Church congregation and membership—committing to a local church family.

- Affinity groups—growing together with others like you: men, women, singles, teens, motorcyclists, senior citizens, and so on.

- Bible study groups—regular meetings to learn the scriptures together

- Service and mission groups—choir, neighborhood and community projects, compassion and evangelism efforts, crisis response, and so on.

As iron sharpens iron, so one person sharpens another. (Proverbs 27:17 NIV)

The Method of Christ-Followers

Discipleship is passed on through a simple three-step process: Invite → Invest → Involve. This model applies to all aspects of Christian leadership. When we embrace this process, we help others grow in the Lord.

1. **Invite**

   - Choose—Be intentional in reaching out.

   - Challenge—Encourage full commitment to Christ.

   - Cherish—Show care and investment in their lives.

   "Come, follow me," Jesus said, "and I will send you out to fish for people." (Matthew 4:19 NIV)

2. **Invest**

   - Intercede—Pray regularly for and with those you are discipling.

   - Instruct—Teach them to walk with Jesus.

   - Introduce—Connect them with Christ, the Holy Spirit, and the church community.

   "What you have heard from me in the presence of many witnesses entrust to faithful men, who will be able to teach others also." (2 Timothy 2:2)

3. **Involve**

- Serve—Engage in ministry alongside them.

- Send—Encourage them to step into leadership.

- Supervise—Provide feedback and encouragement.

"Go therefore and make disciples of all nations." (Matthew 28:19)

To make disciples…
- **Invite**
- **Invest**
- **Involve**

Practical Expressions of Leadership

How can we actively step into Christian leadership?

- Lead a small group—Invest in discipling others.

- Mentor a new believer or volunteer—Help guide someone in his or her faith and service journey.

- Step into a leadership role in your local congregation.

- Volunteer for a mission trip—Invite someone to accompany you.

- Serve in a ministry—Use your gifts to bless others.

- Provide compassionate care for the sick, grieving, and suffering.
- Intentionally make relationships with people who are new to the faith or the church

Reflection and Application

1. Reflect: Who has discipled you, and who are you discipling?

2. Ask: Are there Christians in my life farther down the road in faith than me? Name a few. Are there those (Christian and non-Christian) who are behind me on the road of discipleship? Name some of those.

3. Act: Take an intentional step toward leadership—invite, invest, or involve.

4. Pray: Ask God to shape you into a leader who makes disciples.

Are you ready to lead? Leadership in Christ's kingdom is not about power or position—it is about serving and sharing influence.

CONCLUSION

WALKING THE DISCIPLES' PATH

Discipleship is not a **destination** but rather a **lifelong journey**. As a compass guiding a traveler, the **Disciples' Compass** helps us navigate the path of faith, ensuring we are always moving **toward Christ**. Worship, relationship, discipleship, citizenship, partnership, and leadership—each of these points leads us more deeply into our calling as followers of Jesus.

When we set our **pivot point** in worship, we acknowledge that **everything begins with God**. Then our relationship extends our connection **horizontally**—we grow in community with other believers. Discipleship leads us **upward**, shaping our lives. Citizenship takes our faith **outward**, impacting the world around us. Partnership unites our efforts, increasing our results. And leadership multiplies our influence, making **disciples who make disciples**.

The challenge before us is clear: **Will we follow?**

> **"If anyone would come after me, let him deny himself and take up his cross and follow me."** (Matthew 16:24)

While there are times to be still, to reflect, to rest, and to renew, Jesus did not call us to **stationary lives.** He called us to **move**. Our faith should be dynamic. As with the **first disciples**, we are invited to follow Him, not just for our own salvation but also to **bring others along on the journey**.

Each of us must examine ourselves based on these compass points. Are we mere spectators or are we participants in our spiritual development?

Now is the time to commit. **The compass is in your hand. Will you follow?**

THE COMPASS COVENANT

I covenant with God to follow the Disciples' Compass:

I.   **I will *Know God in Worship***

- I believe that Jesus Christ is my *Savior*, and I have assurance of the forgiveness of my sins.

- I confess Jesus Christ as the *Lord* of my life.

- I will develop and nurture a life of surrender to and worship of God.

- I will be faithful in my attendance at weekly services of worship.

II. **I will *Show Love in Relationship***

- I will become involved in the lives of others by being a part of a local church and by joining a small group of believers for prayer, outreach, inspiration, nurture, and teaching.

- I will act only in loving ways toward others, refusing to gossip or speak negatively about others.

III. **I will *Grow Up in Discipleship***

- I commit to a life of spiritual growth through regular prayer, Bible study, devotion, personal and public worship, obedience, faith, service, and love.

- Baptism:

  - ___ I affirm that I have been baptized in water for the remission of sins, or…

  - ___ I agree to be baptized on_____ (date)

- I will participate in discipleship training programs as possible.

- I seek to be entirely set apart for God and be filled with His Spirit.

IV. **I will *Go Out in Citizenship***

- I will live a godly life, being the best citizen I can be at home, at work, and everywhere I go.

- I will seek ways to serve my community and world.

- I will practice deeds of compassion and generosity for the poor, sick, bereaved, and downcast.

V. **I will *Sow Seeds of Partnership***

- *Pray*: I will regularly pray with and for my church and fellow members and attendees.

- *Serve*: I agree to be equipped to serve by my pastors and teachers; I will develop a servant's heart;

I agree to serve in the following identifiable and accountable ministries: _____

_____

_____

_____

_____

_____

_____

- *Invite*: I will invite un-churched people to attend and inactive attendees to return to our fellowship.

- *Give*: I will practice biblical stewardship by bringing my tithe into the storehouse and by giving sacrificially as God leads.

VI. **I will *Flow On to Leadership***

- As I grow in Christ, I will disciple others to follow Him, passing on the faith that was given to me.

- I will obey the call of God to serve in leadership roles in my church and to participate in subsequent training as required by the position of leadership that I assume.

- I commit to follow the leadership in place by God's assignment and the church's affirmation.

Signed: _____ **Date:** _____

ABOUT THE AUTHOR

SCOTT WADE is the founder of Momentum Ministries, a nonprofit organization dedicated to helping individuals and churches attain, maintain, and regain spiritual momentum. With a deep passion for discipleship, preaching, and writing, Scott has spent decades equipping believers to live as followers of Christ.

An ordained elder in the Church of the Nazarene, Scott has served as a pastor, evangelist, author, and mentor, ministering to churches across the United States. After nearly thirty years of pastoral ministry, he felt called to "get out of the boat" and launch Momentum Ministries, expanding his impact through books, preaching, and leadership development. His weekly podcast, *Casual Conversations*, by Momentum Ministries, and his daily devotional blog, *Daily Momentum,* continue to encourage believers in their faith journeys.

Scott and his wife, Lana, reside on Johns Island, South Carolina. They have three daughters, three sons-in-law, and twelve grandchildren who bring joy to their lives. When not writing or preaching, Scott enjoys traveling, mentoring, and partnering with churches to bring revival and renewal.

To connect with Scott or explore his other books and resources, visit *momentumministries.org*.

OTHER BOOKS BY SCOTT WADE

Christmas with Luke (English, Spanish, and Portuguese)
Christmas with Matthew (English and Spanish)
Proverbs: Wisdom for the Way (English and Spanish)

The Climb: A five-year devotional guide through the Bible
    Book 1: *Start Here*
    Book 2: *Stay Focused*
    Book 3: *Stick with It*
    Book 4: *Stretch Yourself*
    Book 5: *Stand Tall*
    Book 6: *Still Waters: Devotions from the Psalms*

How to order:
Visit the Momentum Ministries website at
www.momentumministries.org
to order copies of these and other books to help you
attain, maintain, and regain spiritual momentum.